WARSHIP PICTORIAL #27
Kriegsmarine Type VII

by Steve Wiper

U-251 *at Narvik in June 1942.*

CLASSIC WARSHIPS PUBLISHING

P. O. Box 57591 • Tucson, AZ. 85732 • USA
Web Site: www.classicwarships.com • Ph/Fx (520)748-2992
Copyright © August 2004
ISBN 0-9745687-6-7
Printed by Arizona Lithographers, Tucson, Arizona

1

General History of the Kriegsmarine Type VII U-boats

After the end of the Great War, the Treaty of Versailles in 1919 dictated that Germany would no longer have U-boats in her navy and was not allowed to pursue any development or have experimental programs concerning submarines. About 1922, a German financed "Submarine Development Bureau" was formed in Holland in secret, funded by the Reichsmarine. Designs were made for the Turkish and Finnish navies, and by 1932, a submarine for Turkey was built in Spanish shipyards. This was the prototype for the new seagoing submarine of the future German Navy. By 1934, enough materials had been purchased in Spain, Holland and Finland to start work on 10 submarines in Germany in anticipation of the denunciation of the Versailles Treaty.

When Hitler announced to the world that Germany would no longer abide by the Treaty of Versailles, Grossadmiral Raeder had made rapid progress on the construction of the new German U-boat fleet. Before the end of 1935, twenty-four of the new U-boats were under construction. These were the Type I oceangoing and Type II coastal. Designs for others were also under development, but the most versatile turned out to be a modification to the Type II design, which was called Type VII.

The Type VII submarines, sometimes called VIIA, submarine proved to be a much better sea boat than the Type I in test runs during 1936, ten of which were built and completed by 1937. These boats, designed in secret during 1933-1934, were the first of a new generation of German attack U-boats, popular with their crews and very agile on the surface. They also had a much more powerful striking force than the smaller Type II. They had five torpedo tubes, four in the bow and one astern and could carry eleven torpedoes onboard or 22 TMA (33 TMB) mines. These Type VII submarines had a unique feature of the stern mounted torpedo tube being external and mounted on the aft deck. They also had an effective 88mm fast-firing deck gun with 160 rounds of ammunition. Except for *U-29* and *U-30* scuttled in Kupfermühlen Bay on May 4, 1945, all Type VII U-boats were sunk during the Second World War.

Soon it was discovered that the only real drawback of the Type VII was its small fuel storage. This was mostly rectified in the VIIB, which had an additional 33 tons of fuel in external saddle tanks providing additional range of about 2500nm at 10 knots. This was accomplished by lengthening the submarine by 2m (6.56 ft.), with the displacement increasing from 500 to 517 tons. They were also considerably more powerful and slightly faster than the Type VII. They had turbochargers added to the diesel engines for a 20% increase in power. These boats, and all following designs, had two rudders instead of the one found on the VII, giving them even more agility. They also had the same armament as the VII, four bow torpedo tubes and one tube at the stern. In this design, the stern tube was fitted below water, between the rudders. *U-83* was the only type VIIB without the stern torpedo tube. The only major armament difference was that three additional torpedoes could be stored for a total of fourteen. Type VIIB U-boats included many of the most famous U-boats during World War II, including Kretschmer's *U-99*, *U-48*, the most successful U-boat of the war, Prien's *U-47* and Schepke's *U-100*. Twenty-four of these boats were constructed, with only four surviving the war, three of which were scuttled at the wars end.

The next development of this series was the mass produced Type VIIC with several improvements over the Type VIIB. They had basically the same engine layout and power, but were slightly larger and heavier making them not quite as fast as the VIIB. They were once again lengthened by 0.6m (2 ft.) to accommodate underwater sound detection gear. The conning tower was also lengthened by 0.3m (1 ft.) and widened slightly. The installation of pressure-proof buoyancy regulating tanks, port and starboard, helped to improve rough weather seakeeping abilities. The fuel capacity was again increased by 4.5 tons with slightly larger saddle tanks. An engine oil cleaning system was also installed. The torpedo tube arrangement was the same as the VIIB, except in the following boats. Only two bow tubes were installed in *U-72*, *U-78*, *U-80*, *U-554* and *U-555*, and no stern tube in *U-203*, *U-331*, *U-351*, *U-401*, *U-431* and *U-651*. The VII C

was the workhorse of the German U-boat fleet in World War Two from 1941 onwards and boats of this type were built throughout the war. The first VIIC boat commissioned was the *U-69* in 1940. The VIIC was an effective fighting machine and was seen in almost all areas where the U-boat fleet operated. The VIIC came into service as the "Happy Days" were ending and it was this boat that faced the Allied anti-submarine campaign in late 1943 and 1944 leading to final defeat. Perhaps the most famous VIIC boat was *U-96*. Other noticeable boats were the U-flak boats. Many of these Type VIIC U-boats were fitted with the Schnorkel in 1944-1945. There were a total of 593 U-boats of the Type VIIC variation constructed before and during the war, with only 136 surviving, fifty of those scuttled by their crews at the end of hostilities.

The next evolution of the Type VII was the Type VIIC/41. This variation was designed from experiences learned during the first two years of the war, comprising a slightly modified version of the successful VII C, with basically the same engine layout and power. Torpedo armament was the same with five tube arrangement. The major difference was that these boats had a stronger pressure hull giving them more depth to evade attack. Their operational depth increased from 100m (328 ft.) to 120m (393.6 ft.) and crush depth from 200 (656 ft.) to 250m (820 ft.). They also had lighter machinery to compensate for the added steel thickness, 21mm compared to 18.5mm in the hull, making them actually slightly lighter than the VII C. All the type VII C/41 boats from *U-1271* onwards had the mine fittings deleted. This design saw further change in the much improved type VII C/42 but none of those were ever completed, being canceled in favor of the Type XXI Elektro boat in late 1943. The first of the VII C/41 U-boats were delivered in August 1943. Of the 70 built, 44 survived the war, with 18 of those scuttled by their crews in early May 1945. One Type VII C/41, *U-995* still exists today, on display at Laboe, north of Kiel, Germany, and is also the only surviving Type VII.

The larger minelaying Type VIID was a direc

variant of the VIIC. These boats, designed in 1939-1940, and constructed 1940-1942, were basically a longer version of the type VIIC with five additional SMA mine shafts just aft of the conning tower. Fifteen additional mines were carried in these shafts. These U-boats were 9.8m (32 ft.) longer amidships, which also meant they had longer saddle tanks and carried more fuel and therefore had an extended range. They were armed with same five torpedo tube configuration, carrying 12 torpedoes or 26 SMA mines (39 TMB) and had the 88mm deck gun with 220 rounds. These boats did not fare very well with only one out of six surviving the war. The other five were sunk with all hands, a total of 241 men perishing.

Another variant of the VII attack U-boats was the large Type VIIF torpedo transport U-boats. There were four of these submarines, designed in 1941, constructed in 1941-1943, primarily built as torpedo transports and never fitted with the typical 88mm deck guns found on other Type VII boats. They had the traditional five torpedo tube configuration and as attack boats they would carry 14 torpedoes but in their transport role they would have up to 39 torpedoes onboard. Two of them, *U-1062* and *U-1059*, were sent to support the Monsun Type IX U-boats in the Far East waters. Only one of the four of this type built survived the war. They were the largest and heaviest Type VII boats built.

At the beginning of the war, the U-boat crews added a pair of type 151 machine guns to the conning tower for added anti-aircraft protection. The 88mm deck gun was very useful in sinking merchantmen, enabling the more expensive torpedoes to be saved for larger and more valuable targets. For the most part, the U-boats were free to roam the seas in search of merchant shipping and warship targets. Many of the great successes of the war were scored early in this conflict, including the sinking of the British Royal Navy aircraft carrier *HMS Courageous* and the battleship *HMS Royal Oak*.

By early 1940, with moderate losses, the German U-boats were having a great effect upon the British supply line. As the U-boats developed their tactics between March and November 1940, Allied shipping losses rose to 1,600,000 tons, even as the British re-established the convoy system used in the Great War. By

this time, the latest tactic was for a U-boat to trim down until only the conning tower was above water and to penetrate the columns of a convoy at night, enabling the boat to fire her torpedoes with impunity, while the convoy's escort was on the flank and nowhere near the attacking submarine. The only British counter-measure for this at the time was to fire "Snowflake" rockets to illuminate the convoy and hope to spot the attacking U-boat.

By October 1940, the German Navy had developed a new tactic, known as the "Wolf Pack" technique. This enabled new submarine commanders and crews to survive long enough to gain valuable experience and increased the odds of success by attacking a convoy with large numbers of U-boats, overwhelming the escort. By March 1941, this tactic was used in almost all U-boat offenses. During that month, however, the British convoy escorts sank three of Germany's top U-boat aces, Prien *U-47*, Kretschmer *U-99* and Schepke *U-100*. This was a heavy blow to the Kriegsmarine, as all three had sunk 111 ships, totaling over 500,000 tons. They had fallen victims to new weapons and tactics. Also in late 1940 and early 1941, the aft end of the conning tower on some Type VII U-boats was enlarged to accommodate an additional single 20mm AA mount. Aircraft began to become a major problem at this point in the Battle of the Atlantic, as it became known. In May 1941, a British boarding party on the damaged *U-110* managed to capture a German code machine known as the Enigma Cypher, enabling the Royal Navy to read all the German Naval codes. This was one of the greatest victories for the Allies throughout the war. Towards the end of 1941, the British developed a high frequency receiver that could locate a shadowing U-boat, making convoy tracking difficult. The British also managed to develop a surface warning radar, type 271, small enough to be mounted in the convoy escort Flower class corvette, again making the detection of U-boats easier. Even with all the set backs, the U-boats managed to sink more than 2,000,000 tons of merchant shipping in 1941. To counter the British radar, the U-boats had a system of their own developed in mid-1941. This was the FuMO-29, which was mounted on the face of the conning tower. It was installed in only a few Type VII U-boats. In the last months of 1941, start-

ing in September, six U-boats were sent to the Mediterranean to try to turn the tide of that campaign. Another four were sent in October. On November 13, *U-81* sank the British aircraft carrier *HMS Ark Royal* and on the 25th, *U-331* sank the battleship *HMS Barham*. Also during the later half of 1941, Hitler demanded that the U-boats not attack escorting United States warships, even though they were helping the British with their convoy system. U-boat commanders were frustrated by this, but still three US Navy destroyers were attacked, one damaged and one sunk. After the Japanese attack upon Pearl Harbor on December 7th., Hitler declared war upon the United States and lifted restrictions on attacks on American shipping on December 9, 1941.

The year 1942 was a pivotal time for the Battle of the Atlantic. Germany's Admiral Dönitz knew that if he could sink 800,000 tons of shipping per month he could isolate England from the economic might of the United States, thereby winning the war in the west and possibly the entire conflict. The tonnage of Allied shipping sunk at the beginning of 1942 was averaging 650,000 tons per month. By mid-1942, the US Navy was able to provide escort aircraft carriers and in combination with British Very Long Range Liberator anti-submarine patrol aircraft, these factors helped the Allies keep slightly ahead of the U-boats. By September of 1942, the British were able to also form convoy escort support groups of well trained escort destroyers and frigates, which operated independently of the convoy escorts. They were able to spend as much time as necessary hunting down any U-boat to its destruction.

By mid-1942, the 88mm deck gun was not able to be used due to the ever increasing numbers of escort vessels and aircraft attacks, so it was removed as permitted during that year and into 1943. U-boat radar saw an improved FuMO-30 rotating mast replace the fixed antenna of the FuMO-29 "Seetakt" system, but units were not installed until September 1942. The U-boats also had a small rotating mast installed that was a radar receiver, known as FuMB-1 "Metox", sometimes called the "Biscay Cross". By the end of 1942, modifications to the conning tower for enlarged anti-aircraft batteries took place. These were known as Modifications, of which number II was carried out. This was an additional platform aft of the conning tower in the Type VIIB and an extended platform in the Type VIIC, each mounting a single 20mm AA weapon.

In the fall of 1942, the Allies pulled their escort carrier groups from the Atlantic to support the "Torch" landings in North Africa, weakening their submarine hunting efforts and giving the Atlantic U-boats a reprieve. This did have not as great an effect as the Germans hoped for because of a severe winter, but none the less, the U-boats managed to sink 6,000,000 tons of Allied shipping that year.

During the beginning of 1943, the Allies rerouted their convoys, making their location by the U-boats difficult and keeping shipping losses down. Due to the Allied code breakers, the location of U-boat wolf packs was transmitted to convoy escorts and convoys were again rerouted and the hunter-killer groups swooped in on the unsuspecting German submarines. U-boat successes were very low until March. During that month the Germans managed to get their wolf packs in place to attack several convoys, sinking 627,000 tons.

Improvements to the Type VII U-boats during 1943 were Modification III to the conning tower of the Type VIID mine laying boats, a widened bridge platform accommodating a pair of single 20mm AA guns. Mod. IV was also employed on the Type VIIC and the early C/41 U-boats, which were enlarged upper and lower platforms, mounting the new twin 20mm AA gun and the new single 37mm, or quad 20mm AA mounts. By the later months of 1943, nearly all Type VII U-boats had the 88mm deck gun removed, as Allied patrol aircraft made use of this weapon nearly impossible. The few boats that kept this gun operated in the Baltic, where Russian air cover was limited. Radar advances in 1943 with the FuMO-61, a vast improvement over FuMO-30, and installation began late in that year. The FuMB-1 radar receiver was upgraded with the FuG-350 "Naxos", again a great improvement over the previous system, installation beginning in November 1943. Another item introduced to the U-boats was the new acoustic torpedo, designed to be used against the convoy escorts, but was hampered by technical problems early in their introduc-

tion. The last item introduced in 1943 was the radar decoy "Aphrodite", which was a hydrogen filled decoy balloon, anchored a few meters above water, with aluminum streamers to create a strong radar return signal.

By April of 1943, the convoy support groups were back in the Atlantic hunting down the U-boats. U-boat losses spiked to 41 boats sunk in May 1943, while their tonnage sunk fell to a all time low of only 95,000 tons in June. These losses caused the Germans to withdraw all boats from the Atlantic in early June. Building of the Type VII boats was increased to 27 per month from that time. During the summer of 1943 the U-boat arm of the German Navy was also experiencing a severe shortage of new recruits and as submarine crew numbers dwindled due to the increased sinkings, there was an overall shortage of crews. The average life expectancy at this time was now down to three patrols.

During this down time for the U-boats, a new tactic and weapon was introduced by the Germans, the flak trap. These were four "Flak Boats" were fitted with two quadruple 20mm and one 37mm AA weapons to combat patrolling Allied aircraft. They achieved successes against surprised British aircraft, but the effort gave the U-boats only about two months of victories until the British developed counter-measures where they called in surface hunters to assist the aircraft and the Flak Boats were withdrawn and converted back into their previous configurations.

July saw the resumption of U-boat activity in the Atlantic, with moderate gains in tonnage sunk, but not nearly enough to reach the goals Germany's Admiral Dönitz had set to bring England to her knees. August brought another huge series of losses for the U-boats, even worse than the May-June fiasco. Only 86,000 tons of Allied shipping were sunk. The introduction of the new acoustic homing torpedo to fight the convoy escorts did not always function properly, causing the loss of a few boats. To make matters worse, the Allies introduced their own acoustic homing torpedo, "Fido", which worked quite well. By October, the Americans developed "Foxer", a noise making device towed behind an escort to fool the German acoustic torpedo, which led to more U-boat losses. By the end of 1943, the days of the wolf pack

tactics were numbered. During 1943, the U-boats only managed to sink just over 804,000 tons of allied shipping, at a loss of 260 submarines.

In January 1944, U-boat operations were pulled closer to England to prey on Allied shipping as they neared their home ports. In February the "Schnorkel" was introduced to the U-boats, making their detection harder for Allied escorts and hunter-killer groups. This device allowed the U-boats to run their diesel engines, charge batteries and vent the boats with fresh air while running submerged. The schnorkel rose above the surface by only a meter, but the U-boat could only move at slow speed and the wake was easy to spot during the daylight hours. As a result of this, the Allied hunter-killer groups were quite successful, sinking 60 U-boats between January and March 1944, while losing 328,000 tons of shipping. The Americans developed another device by this time called "MAD" short for magnetic anomaly detector, that could spot a submerged submarine from an aircraft. Yet another anti-submarine device introduced at this time was the sonar buoy, which the US Navy used with success in the central Atlantic, starting in March.

The German Navy was sending out their U-boats as much as possible to try to stem the ever increasing tide of Allied advances, but the writing was on the wall for the U-boats. The Allied bombing campaign was also putting a severe restriction on new construction and repairs. Germany's Admiral Dönitz was trying to hold off eventual defeat, in hope of getting new U-boat designs into service by the end of 1944. The problem here was that they were trying to develop four completely new concept designs, only two of which were feasible, thereby wasting an incredible amount of effort, instead of working on one reasonable design, the Type XXI. This caused the cancellation of the last evolution of the Type VII, called the VIIC/42, which was to have a thicker steel pressure hull, increased AA weapons, schnorkel, and the latest electronic warfare equipment. To extend the life of the Type VII U-boats, the AA was further improved with the Modification V and VI, an addition of a forward sponson or platform mounting anything from a single or twin 20mm, to a single or twin 37mm, or even a quadruple 20mm AA weapon. These proved to make the U-boa unstable, especially with the larger weapons, so were fitted only in limited numbers. Radar was improved with the FuMO-61 and radar detection systems were improved with introduction of the "Bali" omni-directional receiver and the "Palau" direction finding radar.

In June, during the Normandy landings, the U-boat arm tried to penetrate the D-Day invasion force, but only managed to sink one LST nine days after D-Day, at the loss of six submarines. Within a couple of months, the French bunkers and ports were abandoned by the U-boat arm of the German Navy, with the U-boats going to Germany and Norway. Escort forces and the hunter-killer groups were working so effectively that during the later half of 1944, not one single merchant ship steaming for Murmansk, Russia was sunk. By the middle of 1944, all U-boats in the Mediterranean were destroyed, or had escaped to the Atlantic, ending that theater of operations. Some success for the U-boats was obtained around the British Isles, but with only meager tonnage amounts compared to early war totals, and at the cost of numerous U-boats sunk. The Germans lost 239 submarines, and sank just 359,000 tons of Allied shipping during the year of 1944.

By the end of 1944 and the first month of 1945, Allied escort forces were built up to a very large number around the British Isles, so much so that the U-boats were virtually unable to penetrate their screen, losing huge numbers of submarines and sinking very few merchant ships. More and more of the U-boats were steaming for Norway, which was difficult for British bombers to reach and was therefore the safest base from which to operate. During the last month of the war, April, a huge exodus of U-boats, personnel and supplies were headed for Norway. Allied aircraft were furiously attacking these submarines, taking a heavy toll, with the final number of U-boats sunk during the four months of war during 1945 at 153. Still the U-boats somehow managed to sink 282,000 tons of Allied shipping.

Admiral Dönitz, by that time the new Reich President appointed by Hitler (who then committed suicide) sent out the surrender signal to all 43 U-boats at sea on May 4, 1945 to cease hostilities and set course for an authorized port of surrender. At first the submarine commanders refused, but soon after a radio speech from Dönitz praising them for their efforts against an overwhelming enemy, they each surfaced and sailed to the designated ports. All except two, one of which, U-977, a Type VIIC, evaded Allied warships and schnorkeled for Argentina, arriving weeks after the end of hostilities.

The U-boat arm of the German Navy suffered the largest losses of that force, losing 784 submarines, of which 519 were Type VII variants, and a total of over 28,000 men. All U-boats managed to sink 2,603 merchant ships, totaling over 13.5 million tons, and 175 Allied warships. An estimated 700 Allied aircraft were destroyed, or damaged too badly to fly again by U-boats during the war. For this, about 220 U-boats were sunk directly by Allied aircraft. The Type VII boats were state of the art submarines at the beginning of the Second World War, but due to advances in many technologies, Allied strategic bombing, and arrogance on the part of the the German leadership, these boats were woefully inadequate by mid-war. Their production in large numbers and reliability was the reason for their continued, but dwindling successes. By 1944, they were death traps for their crews, whose life span had dwindled to merely two patrols at best.

This drawing of an interior profile view of a Type VIIC is from a set of captured documents, copied from the US Naval Technical Mission to Europe files.

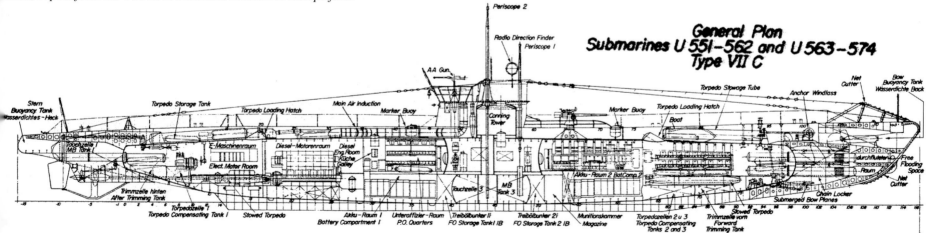

Type VII U-boat

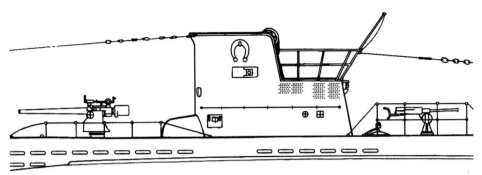

Displacement:(tons)	626 surfaced, 745 submerged, 915 total.
Length: (m)	64.51 (211.6 ft.) overall, 45.5 (149.25 ft.) pressure hull.
Beam: (m)	5.85 (19.19 ft.) overall, 4.7 (15.42 ft.) pressure hull.
Draught: (m)	4.37 (14.33 ft.).
Height: (m)	9.5 (31.16 ft.).
Power: (hp)	2310 surfaced, 750 submerged.
Speed:(knots)	17 surfaced, 8 submerged.
Range:(miles / knots)	6200/10 surfaced, 94/4 submerged.
Torpedoes:	11 (4 bow & 1 stern tubes).
Mines:	22 TMA or 33 TMB.
Deck gun:	1 x 88mm/45cal. C/35 mount with 160 rounds.
Anti-aircraft gun:	1 x 20mm C/30 mount with 1100 rounds.
Crew:	42-46 men.
Max depth:(m)	ca. 220 (722 feet).

This image of U-28 was taken about 1938 in the Baltic, while the lower image is of U-27, with the aft torpedo tube visible in the stern, also taken before the Second World War.

Another image of U-28, taken in Spain during the Spanish Civil War, about 1937. Note the neutrality stripes painted on the conning tower. See page 32 for a color illustration.

The image below is of an experimental forward sponson for anti-aircraft guns on U-33, about 1939.

This image is of a Type VII U-boat at sea, on patrol early in the war. Note the small size of the conning tower.

Above is a photograph of U-33 during her sortie to Spanish waters during that civil war, with the black, white and red neutrality stripes on the conning tower. The image to the right looking down onto the conning tower of U-34 during her first year of the Second World War, shows her victory flags of sunken merchantmen. Below is a photograph of U-30, U-31, and U-32 at Hamburg during the winter months in 1938. Note the smooth surface of the face of the conning tower during the pre-war years.

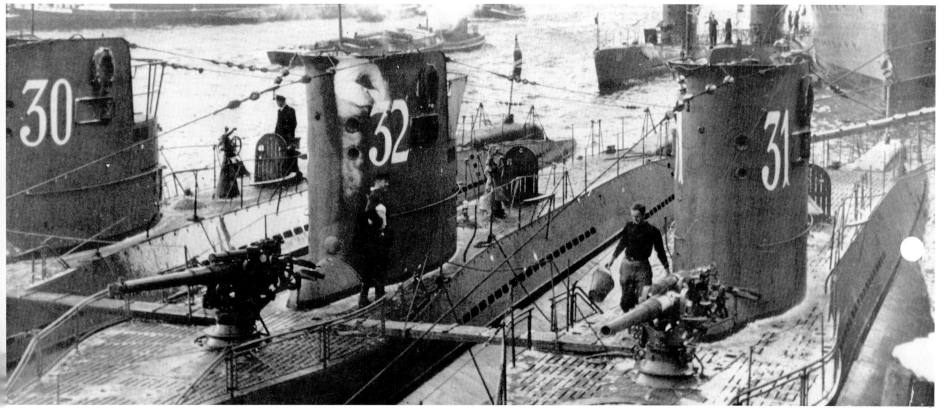

Two slightly different variants of the Type VII U-boat are seen here in this image, taken in the early months of 1940, during the war. The submarine closest to the camera was U-29, while the other was U-30. U-29 still mounted her 20mm AA gun on the main deck aft of the conning tower, while U-30 had hers mounted on the enlarged aft conning tower platform. Note that both submarines still have no breakwater fitted to the face and sides of the conning tower. Note also the vent holes in the sides of the conning tower of both boats.

The photograph to the left is of the U-29, which operated out of Norway, this image taken sometime in 1941. She still had the smooth surface on the conning tower at that time. Below is the fore deck of a Type VII U-boat headed back to port. Note the retractable bollards are in their extended position on the port side. The submarines 88mm deck gun is visible in the foreground of this image. The cylindrical objects on the rigging running towards the bow are insulators for the radio antenna.

Type VIIB U-boat

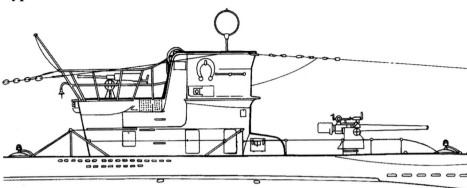

Displacement:(tons)	753 surfaced, 857 submerged, 1040 total.
Length: (m)	66.5 (218.1 ft.) overall, 48.8 (160 ft.) pressure hull.
Beam: (m)	6.2 (20.34 ft.) overall, 4.7 (15.42 ft.) pressure hull.
Draught: (m)	4.74 (15.55 ft.).
Height: (m)	9.5 (31.16 ft.).
Power: (hp)	3200 surfaced, 750 submerged.
Speed:(knots)	18 surfaced, 8 submerged.
Range:(miles / knots)	8700/10 surfaced, 90/4 submerged.
Torpedoes:	14 (4 bow & 1 stern tubes).
Mines:	26 TMA or 39 TMB.
Deck gun:	1 x 88mm/45cal. C/35 mount with 220 rounds.
Anti-aircraft gun:	1 x 20mm C/30 mount with 1100 rounds.
Crew:	42-46 men.
Max depth:(m)	ca. 220 (722 feet).

The image above is of the U-45 running her machinery trials about October 1938, in Kiel Bay. She was the first of the new Type VIIB U-boats, built at the Krupp Germaniawerft Shipyards in Kiel, Germany. As one can see by the statistics listed above, the VIIB was a slightly modified version of the previous design, the main difference was being the stern torpedo tube mounted underwater, between the new twin rudder configuration. The white lines painted on the hull were to measure the bow wake during speed trials.

This photograph is of the U-46 returning to home port after her collision with her target! She had fired her torpedo and followed it to the target. The ship, having gone dead in the water from the torpedo hit, was in the path of the U-boat which did not observe the target and was running shallow, thereby colliding with the merchant ship. This put her out of commission for quite some time until the conning tower could be repaired. She was then used as a training U-boat in the Baltic for cadets. By the emblem on the conning tower, she was one of the boats in the 7th Flotilla, based at St. Nazaire, France. This emblem was originally that of U-47, commanded by Gunther Prien, famous for sneaking into the main British naval base at Scapa Flow and sinking the battleship HMS Royal Oak. *After his later loss in the convoy battles in the Atlantic, the Flotilla adopted his emblem as theirs.*

Both of the images on this page are of the famous U-47. The smaller inset photo is of her conning tower with its famous emblem and the tonnage sunk at the time the photo was taken. The main image is of U-47 checking the papers of a merchant ship early in the war, prior to her sinking the battleship HMS Royal Oak. Note the marker buoy hatch on the foredeck and the net cutter on the bow.

The two images on the left show the process of reloading torpedoes into the U-boat. This was done using a special slide down through a deck hatch into the submarine. The image above is of the U-48 returning from an early war patrol with her victory pennants flying. The image below is of the U-53 training her crew on the 88mm deck gun.

This photograph below is of the famous U-100, taken about 1940, early in the war. This boat and its crew was lost to Allied convoy escorts while it participated in a wolf pack attack on an Atlantic convoy during March 1941.

U-73, pictured here during 1943, was painted in an overall dunkelgrau, or dark gray. This photograph is a good view of the vent holes in this area of the deck of the Type VIIB U-boat.

Another image of U-73, this one photographed at Lorient, France, her base of operations for the Atlantic with the 7th U-boat Flotilla. The cables wrapped around periscope #2 were to break up the wake left by that device while the boat was sub- *merged. Equipment on the conning tower varied from boat to boat due to their manufacture at different shipyards. Compare this closeup with others throughout the book.*

Both of the photographs on this page were taken during the same rendezvous in the Baltic Sea with U-101 and a support ship. These photos were probably taken while this boat was training cadets in early 1943. She would survive the war, to be scuttled in May 1945. Note that she retained her net cutter and 88mm deck gun to this date.

The image to the left is an aerial view of the bridge on the conning tower of the U-86, showing the 20mm AA mount on its platform and details inside the bridge shield. In the image above, the torpedo aimer is seen, with a pair of waterproof binoculars mounted on top. The coordinates were automatically transmitted down to the command center, which enabled firing solutions to be plotted much quicker. The lower image is of U-52 leaving Lorient, France en route to her patrol in the Atlantic Ocean. Note the molded side of the conning tower. Also, the conning tower was painted with dunkelgrau (dark gray), while the hull above waterline was painted hellgrau (light gray).

Type VIIC U-boat

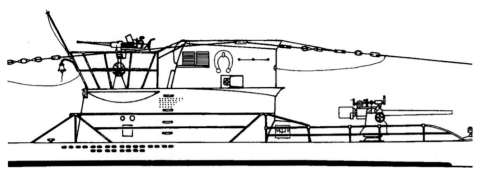

Displacement:(tons)	769 surfaced, 871 submerged, 1070 total.
Length: (m)	67.1 (220.08 ft.) overall, 50.5 (165.64 ft.) pressure hull.
Beam: (m)	6.2 (20.34 ft.) overall, 4.7 (15.42 ft.) pressure hull.
Draught: (m)	4.74 (15.55 ft.).
Height: (m)	9.6 (31.5 ft.).
Power: (hp)	3200 surfaced, 750 submerged.
Speed:(knots)	17.7 surfaced, 7.6 submerged.
Range:(miles / knots)	8500/10 surfaced, 80/4 submerged.
Torpedoes:	14 (4 bow & 1 stern tubes).
Mines:	26 TMA or 39 TMB.
Deck gun:	1 x 88mm/45cal. C/35 mount with 220 rounds.
Anti-aircraft gun:	1 x 20mm C/30 mount with 1100 rounds.
Crew:	44-52 men.
Max depth:(m)	ca. 220 (722 feet).

This photo is of the U-203 arriving at Brest, France in July 1942. She was painted with an overall dunkelgrau (dark gray) above waterline. Note the Olympic rings painted on the face of the conning tower to show support of the 1936 event in Berlin.

The two images on this page show both the face (U-72) and aft end (U-71) of the conning tower of a Type VIIC U-boat. These boats were fitted with the breakwater on the face of conning tower, as well as the wind deflector at the top of the shield of that structure.

Two additional views of the conning towers of Type VIIC U-boats. The image on the left is of U-201 at Brest, France, about 1941. Note the camouflage pattern. The image on the right is an unidentified Type VIIC departing Trondheim, Norway, about 1942.

U-552, commanded by the famous Eric Topp, departing in the left image and arriving in the right image at her base in St. Nazaire, France. Note the battle damage holes in the shield of the conning tower in the right image.

The photographs on this and the previous page are all of a Type VIIB U-boat and a Type IX in the drydock at Lorient, France. These images were taken in late 1940, or early 1941. The Type VIIB is quite possibly U-99, commanded by Otto Kretschmer, one of Germany's early high scoring aces, later lost in a convoy battle in 1941. All of the photographs give a good visual image of the shape of the hull of a Type VII boat. Note the use of netting to try to conceal the submarines from Allied air reconnaissance.

Another view of U-99 in drydock at Lorient, France, in late 1940, or early 1941, with a Type IX in the background. Note the arrangement of the keel blocks to support the U-boat in the drydock and the timber to stabilize the vessel.

The photograph on the following page is of a Type VIIC in a floating drydock, more than likely in Germany, possibly Kiel. The lower hull on most U-boats was painted with anthrazitgrau (charcoal gray), as seen in this photo. The items marked "UT" in that photo were the Unterwasser Telegraphie, which was an underwater telegraph system for U-boats to communicate with each other while in close proximity. The items marked GHG were Gruppenhorrchgerät, or group listening apparatus, or basically hydrophones. Initially there were 11, later, as in this boat, there were 24.

This image is of U-402 about to be launched after completing construction.

This is a good profile view of the conning tower of U-203, a Type VIIC, departing Brest, France. The emblem of the sea turtle represented the one caught and eaten by the crew on an earlier patrol. The emblem was painted in red.

Freiwillig zur

KRIEGSMARINE

The color photograph above was taken during a patrol on a Type VIIB U-boat out in the Atlantic Ocean. It was used in the German propaganda magazine "Signal" during the Second World War.

The color poster to the right was a recruiting tool used by the Kriegsmarine (German Navy) with a Type VIIC U-boat as part of the illustration.

The photo above is of a torpedo being loaded into the submarine while in port.

U-96 loading supplies while in port. The hull above the waterline was painted hellgrau (light gray), while the steel deck was painted with dunkelgrau (dark gray).

The small inset photograph to the right is of a Type VIIC U-boat in arctic waters while hunting Allied convoys bound for Murmansk, Russia. Note that the conning tower has been painted weiß (white) and the deck with dunkelgrau (dark gray), or anthrazitgrau. The 88mm deck gun was often painted dunkelgrau, or schwartz (black), or even a combination of the the two colors, as seen on the deck gun in the primary photo on this page. The main image on this page is of another Type VIIC returning from a battle with the convoy PQ-17, during which the Germans were very successful, sinking many merchant ships. This image was taken sometime in July 1942, at the port of Narvik, Norway. This boat was painted in overall hellgrau (light gray).

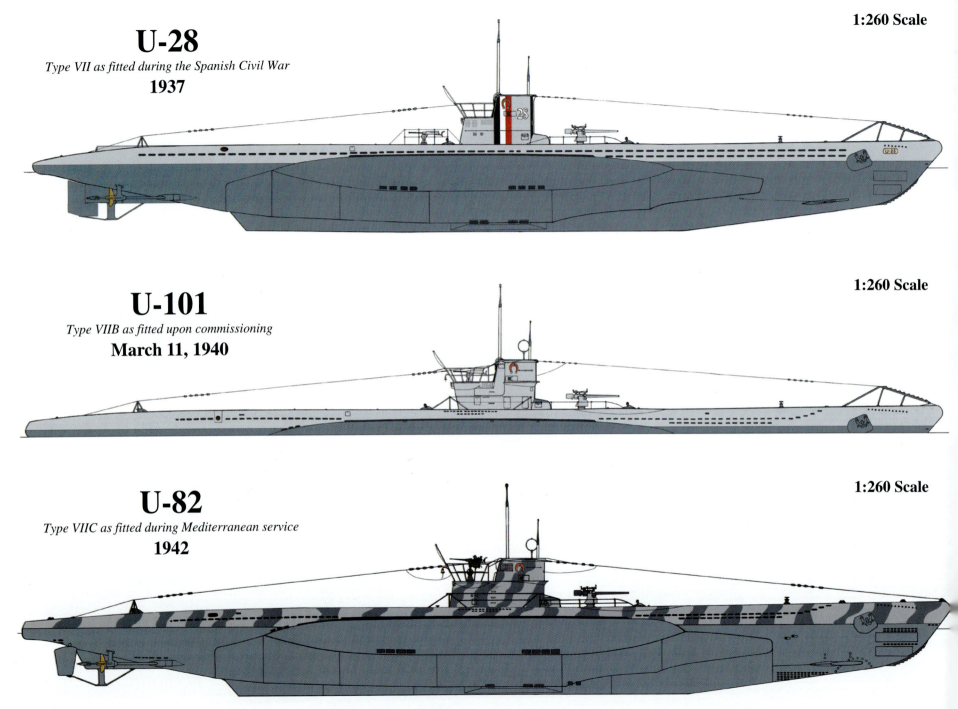

U-28
Type VII as fitted during the Spanish Civil War
1937

1:260 Scale

U-101
Type VIIB as fitted upon commissioning
March 11, 1940

1:260 Scale

U-82
Type VIIC as fitted during Mediterranean service
1942

1:260 Scale

This rare color image of a rather peaceful view of a Type VIIC U-boat tied up at a stone pier was taken during the summer of 1942, somewhere on the Baltic coast, possibly Danzig. The submarine was U-302, which was training her crew at the time this photo was taken. She was commissioned in June of that year.

The image to the left is of the U-431 upon commissioning day in Danzig at the Schichau Works Boatyard, February 2, 1941. Note that the boat was painted overall mittelgrau (medium gray) above the lower hull anthrazitgrau (charcoal gray). The above photo is of the inside of the shield of the conning tower on U-552, about late 1941, while on patrol in the Atlantic Ocean. The decking on this platform was hardwood grating.

Both of the images on this page are from a series of photos taken aboard the U-552. The small inset photo is of the torpedo director on the conning tower with a pair of waterproof binoculars mounted atop.

The primary photo on this page is of the U-552 headed into one of the large bunkers built at St Nazaire, where she was one of the boats in the 7th U-boat Flotilla, in the early months of 1942.

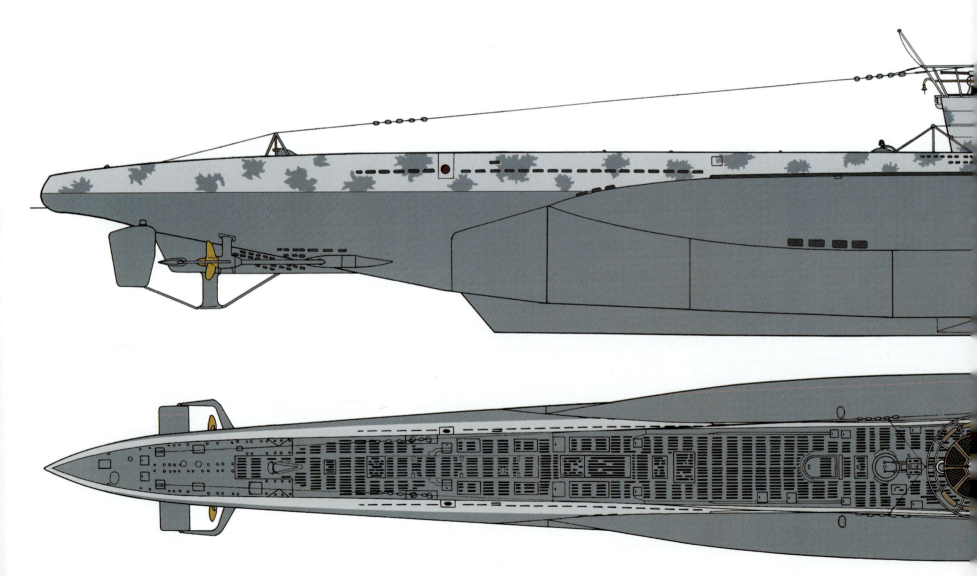

U-83

Camouflage pattern worn while based at La Spezia during 1942. The emblem was of a Viking Long Boat, originally painted on the conning tower while based at Danzig. U-83 was a Type VIIB boat, built by the Flender-Werke Boat Yard at Lübeck, Germany, commissioned in February 1941. This boat was sunk off Oran with all hands by British aircraft on March 9, 1943.

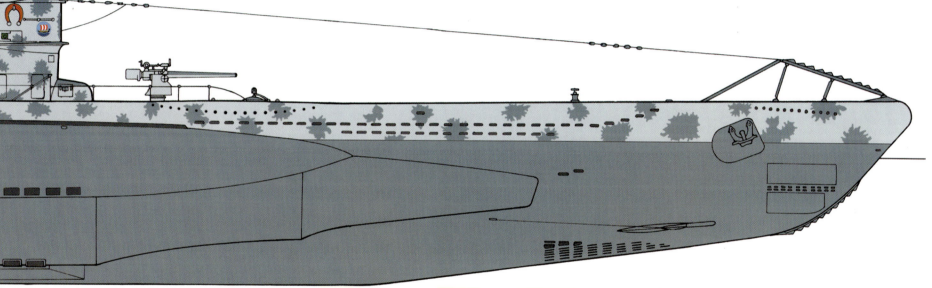

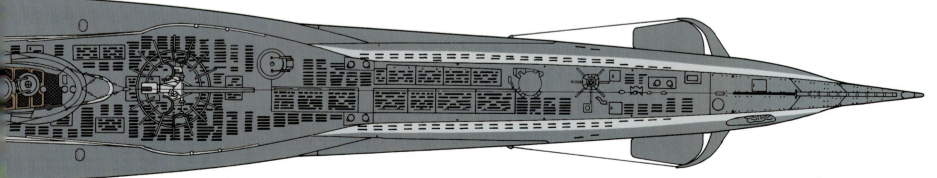

1:126 Scale

The photograph on this page is of one of the few U-boats captured during the Second World War, U-570, seen here at a British port being readied for evaluation. She was later commissioned into the Royal Navy as HMS Graph.

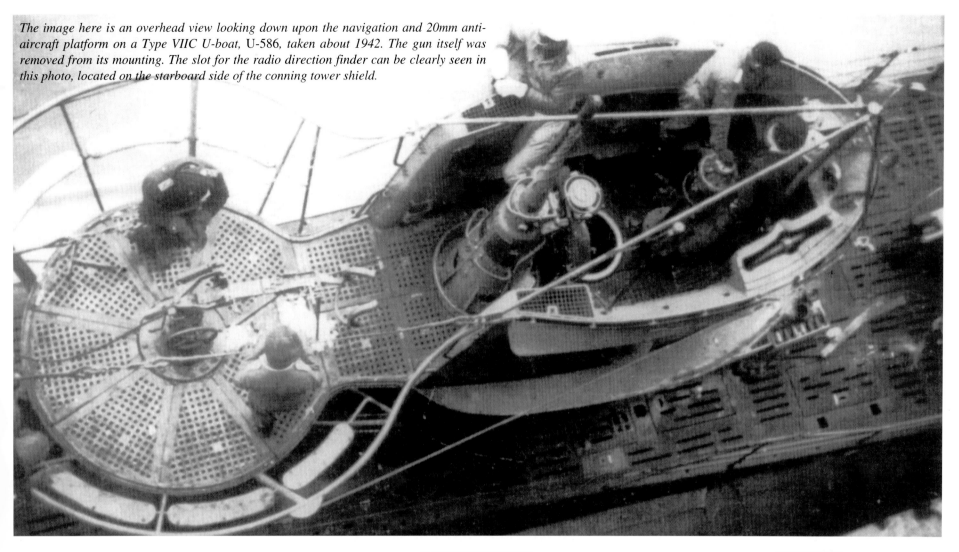

The image here is an overhead view looking down upon the navigation and 20mm anti-aircraft platform on a Type VIIC U-boat, U-586, taken about 1942. The gun itself was removed from its mounting. The slot for the radio direction finder can be clearly seen in this photo, located on the starboard side of the conning tower shield.

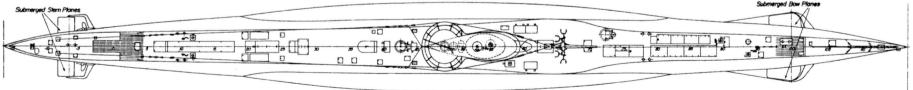

Submerged Stern Planes

Submerged Bow Planes

This drawing of an overhead view of a Type VIIC is from a set of captured documents, copied from the US Naval Technical Mission to Europe files.

Another very rare color photograph from German sources, taken at Gotenhafen, Poland, during the winter of 1940-41. Several Type VII U-boats flank a Type IX, with the target vessel Wega *in the background. The two ships in the foreground are* Donau *and* Bremen. *Note that one of the Type VII boats was painted white.*

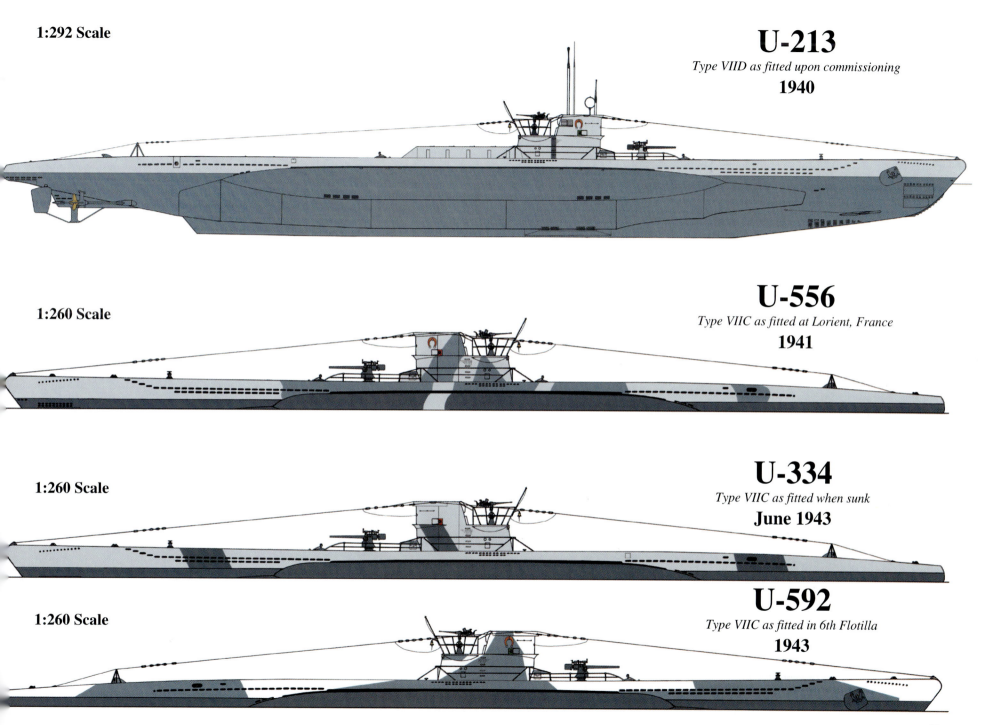

1:292 Scale

U-213
Type VIID as fitted upon commissioning
1940

1:260 Scale

U-556
Type VIIC as fitted at Lorient, France
1941

1:260 Scale

U-334
Type VIIC as fitted when sunk
June 1943

1:260 Scale

U-592
Type VIIC as fitted in 6th Flotilla
1943

Type VIIC/41 U-boat

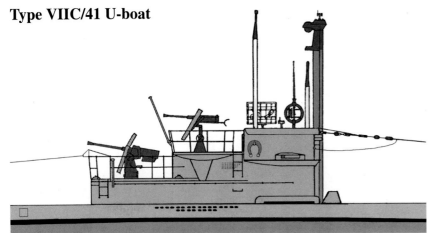

Displacement:(tons)	769 surfaced, 871 submerged, 1070 total.
Length: (m)	67.2 (220.5 ft.) overall, 50.5 (165.64 ft.) pressure hull.
Beam: (m)	6.2 (20.34 ft.) overall, 4.7 (15.42 ft.) pressure hull.
Draught: (m)	4.8 (15.7 ft.).
Height: (m)	9.6 (31.5 ft.).
Power: (hp)	3200 surfaced, 750 submerged.
Speed:(knots)	17.7 surfaced, 7.6 submerged.
Range:(miles / knots)	8500/10 surfaced, 80/4 submerged.
Torpedoes:	14 (4 bow & 1 stern tubes).
Mines:	26 TMA or 39 TMB.
Anti-aircraft guns:	1 x 37mm SKC/30U LC/39 mount w/ 1200 rounds.
	4 x 20mm C/38 twin LM38/43U mounts w/ 4400 rounds.
Crew:	44-52 men.
Max depth:(m)	ca. 220 (722 feet).

U-1023, seen here just after her arrival and surrender to British forces at the conclusion of the Second World War at Weymouth, England.

Above is a very rare photo of U-1168 in 1945 with a 37mm twin FlaK M42U on a LM42U mount fitted on the aft conning tower platform. This was one of the best AA weapons the German Navy designed and built throughout the war, but was rather heavy for the Type VII U-boats. The image above right is of the French "Millé", which was the captured U-471, a Type VIIC, but with the same conning tower configuration as the Type VIIC/41 boats. She had a single 37mm AA mount aft, and also had the 20mm FlaK38 on the LM43U Zwilling (twin) mounting on the upper platform of the conning tower. Below, U-1305 surrendered at sea to a Royal Navy vessel in May 1945.

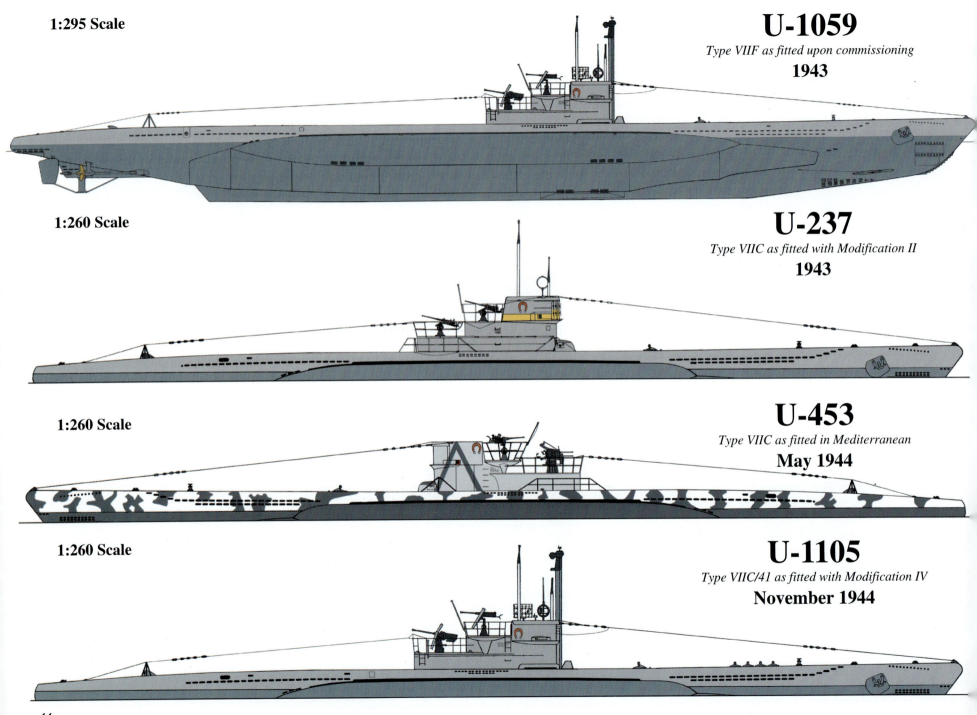

1:295 Scale

U-1059
Type VIIF as fitted upon commissioning
1943

1:260 Scale

U-237
Type VIIC as fitted with Modification II
1943

1:260 Scale

U-453
Type VIIC as fitted in Mediterranean
May 1944

1:260 Scale

U-1105
Type VIIC/41 as fitted with Modification IV
November 1944

Both of the upper photographs are of the U-995, a Type VIIC/41 boat, which is now a museum at Laboe, north of Kiel, Germany. U-995 is the only surviving fully intact example of any of the Type VII U-boat. These photos were taken as she is now, as a museum.

The aerial image to the left is of U-1009 in the Atlantic taken by Allied aircraft during May 1945. The black surrender flag is flying from the periscope, as directed for the safe surrender of all German submarines. She was one of the boats in the 11th U-boat Flotilla, based at Bergen, Norway.

Type VII U-boat Camouflage

The Type VII U-boats used a variety of camouflage patterns throughout the Second World War. Initially, these submarines were painted in an overall *hellgrau* (light gray) above the lower hull color of a number of dark grays, *dunkelblaugrau* (dark blue gray), *anthrazitgrau* (charcoal gray), and most with *shiffsbodenfarbgrau* (ships bottom color gray). Note that on the Type VII U-boats, the bottom color was painted to about one meter above the actual waterline. During the early part of the Second World War, boats operating in Norwegian waters were painted with *weiß* (white) and/or various shades of gray. Boats operating in the Atlantic were usually painted with overall shades of *hellgrau*, or *dunkelgrau* (dark gray) and very few wore patterns of any sort. In the Mediterranean, the application of patterns of dark gray splotches, or bands on top of a lighter gray or white, was very common. Later, as the war turned bad for the German Navy, the U-boats tended to wear an overall camouflage of *dunkelgrau*, or *anthrazitgrau*, giving a very dark appearance, which was hard to spot under water, which is where they spent the majority of their patrols. In almost all cases, throughout the entire war, the deck of the Type VII U-boats was painted *dunkelgrau*, or the same as the lower hull color.

-Note that actual paint chips for the Kriegsmarine can be obtained from Snyder & Short Enterprises, address listed on page 72. They have two sets available.

U-83 returning to port at La Spezia, Italy, where she was part of the 29th U-boat Flotilla in the Mediterranean. She was painted above the lower hull color in overall hellgrau, with anthrazitgrau splotches.

Above are two photos of U-33 (Type VII) wearing an early experimental camouflage pattern of anthrazitgrau and dunkelgrau on a white background. The date is believed to be February 1940, with the 2nd. U-boat Flotilla, based at Wilhelmshaven.

This photo of a Type VIIC boat was taken in one of the French ports. It was one of the few early war pattern camouflages worn in the Atlantic. It was a series of wavy bands of dunkelgrau on a hellgrau background.

This photograph is of the U-404, which had a very unique emblem, in that it was much larger than most, running the length of the conning tower. It was a red Viking ship prow and was painted on both sides of the conning tower. The boat itself was painted in an over-all hellgrau. It was one of the boats of the 6th U-boat Flotilla, based at St. Nazaire, sunk with all hands on July 28, 1943 in the Bay of Biscay. She must also have been one of the first boats to use the schnorkel, the fitting seen on the port side of the conning tower.

The image above is of U-744 departing Brest, France, where she was part of the 9th U-boat Flotilla. The date was about late 1943, or early 1944, prior to her loss in March of that year. She was wearing a pattern camouflage of dunkelgrau wavy bands with soft edges over hellgrau. The 9th Flotilla swordfish emblem was blue with a red mouth.

U-565 *in a rather wild camouflage pattern while she was based at Salamis, Greece with the 29th. U-boat Flotilla. The colors were again dunkelgrau over a hellgrau base paint.*

This photograph is of the U-617 *after she had arrived in the Mediterranean on her transfer to the 29th U-boat Flotilla, based at Pola, on the Italian coast. The splotches on this pattern were painted with anthrazitgrau on a hellgrau base color.*

88mm Deck Gun

This was the secondary weapon on a Type VII U-boat, the primary being the torpedo. Although it was the same calibre as the famous German Army weapon, this naval mount was completely different. This gun was a development of the weapon used by the German Navy during the First World War. The fixed ammunition weight was 21 to 22.5 lbs. per round and could fire about 16 rounds per minute with a well trained crew. Its main function was to be used against small craft, or finish off vessels not sunk with a torpedo, saving that weapon for a more valuable target. Range was 13,000 yards, or about 7.4 miles. Both high explosive (HE @ 21 lbs.) and armor piercing (AP @ 22.5 lbs.) ammunition was available. It was an effective and very reliable weapon.

20mm MG C30 on a LC30/27 mounting was the initial anti-aircraft weapon fitted on the Type VII U-boats. Rate of fire was 280rpm, with a range of 5,250 yards, or 3 miles. The magazine held 20 or 40 rounds of either HE or AP ammunition, both with tracer. The 20mm was the most widely used German gun in the Navy and was very reliable.

The photograph on the previous page is of the U-404, departing St. Nazaire, France and setting out for another hunt for merchant shipping, about 1942. Her 20mm mount is elevated to its highest position. The image to the left was taken of U-96 as she was also departing St. Nazaire, bound for hunting in the Atlantic in July 1941. Above is a illustration from a Kriegsmarine technical manual on the operation of the single 20mm mount. Right, one more image of a 20mm single, this photo with a special tripod mount to stabilize the mount while at sea.

U-707 departing Bordeaux, France on October 12, 1943.

The images on this page and the upper left on the following page pertain to the 20mm FlaK38 with the LM43U Zwilling (twin) mount. This improved version could fire up to 500rpm per barrel at the same range as the MG C30 and using the same ammunition. This mount also had a 12mm thick asymmetrical shield to protect the three to four man crew. This was also a reliable weapon and was a little more capable of bringing down an aircraft due to the volume of fire it could put out. These mounts were fitted to the widened upper platform on the conning tower, but could also be found in the few forward platforms that were built on a limited number of U-boats.

The image here and the illustration in the lower left of this page are of the 37mm FlaK M42U on the LM42U single mounting, which was also manufactured for a twin mounting (see page 43), but those were very rarely fitted, as their weight made the Type VII U-boats slightly unstable. This weapon was capable of firing 180rpm per barrel with a maximum range of 7,200 yards, or 4.1 miles, using AP and HE with tracer ammunition in six round clips. One round from this weapon was capable of bringing down a single engine aircraft, which made it a formidable gun, even against the four engine submarine hunting Liberators.

Quite possibly one of the most feared anti-aircraft weapons by Allied air crews was the German 20mm FlaK38 on the L38/43U Vierling (quadruple) mounting. At 500rpm per barrel, 2000rpm total, this mount could put a large amount of lead up into an oncoming aircraft with catastrophic results for that plane. Some of these weapons were fitted to the aft, lower platform on the Type VII U-boats, in place of the 37mm mounts, but there were four special Type VIIC boats that were converted to test a new tactic, the "Flak Trap". These submarines, U-256, U-441, U-621 and U-953, were all reconfigured with a very large superstructure, mounting a Flak Vierling forward, aft and a single 37mm aft as well. The first boat, U-441, pictured above, was operational in May 1943. These boats were designed to fight it out with Allied patrol and submarine hunting aircraft. The results were mixed. While these boats were able to shoot down attacking aircraft, the Allies concentrated more on these flak boats and their accompanying flock of subs they were trying to escort through the Bay of Biscay. This actually resulted in larger losses against the U-boats. By November 1943, conversion of all four "Flak Boats" was begun to return them to their original configuration.

The images above of the back and front of a flakvierling are from a Office of Naval Intelligence file from the US Navy. The shields were 12mm thick steel. The photo on the lower left of this page is of a Type VIIC boat with a flakvierling on the after platform. Below is an image of U-673, taken about early 1945, with a rare forward platform fitted with a single 37mm FlaK M42U, as well as a pair of twin 20mm mounts on the enlarged conning tower platform and another single 37mm on the after platform.

Type VIID U-boat

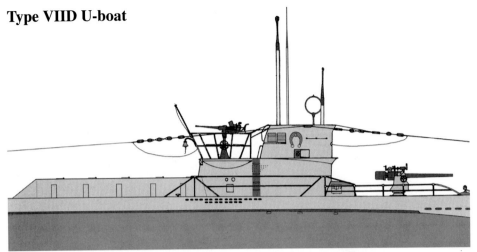

Displacement:(tons)	865 surfaced, 1080 submerged, 1285 total.
Length: (m)	76.90 (252.23 ft.) overall, 59.8 (196.14 ft.) pressure hull.
Beam: (m)	6.38 (20.93 ft.) overall, 4.7 (15.42 ft.) pressure hull.
Draught: (m)	5 (16.4 ft.).
Height: (m)	9.7 (31.8 ft.).
Power: (hp)	3200 surfaced, 750 submerged.
Speed:(knots)	16.7 surfaced, 7.3 submerged.
Range:(miles / knots)	11,200/10 surfaced, 69/4 submerged.
Torpedoes:	14 (4 bow & 1 stern tubes).
Mines:	26 TMA, or 39 TMB *plus* 15 SMA.
Deck Gun:	1 x 88mm SKC35 on LC35 mount w/ 220 rounds.
Anti-aircraft guns:	1 x 20mm C/30 LC30U mount w/ 1100 rounds.
Crew:	46-52 men.
Max depth:(m)	ca. 200 (656 feet).

U-213 in a bunker in one of the French ports used by the Germans as their base of operations for the U-boat war in the Battle of the Atlantic.

The Type VIID U-boat was designed in 1939-40 to be a minelayer, six of which were built, but the larger Type IX and X U-boats filled this role better. The Type VIID were basically a Type VIIC that had a 9.8m (32.14 ft.) section added between frames 39 and 40, aft of the conning tower. This was fitted with five mine tubes, carrying five SMA mines per tube. This extension also included length-ening the saddle tanks, which gave an increased fuel capacity. The boats also carried a schnorkel and had a widened conning tower platform for two 20mm single AA mounts later in the war.

Type VIIF U-boat

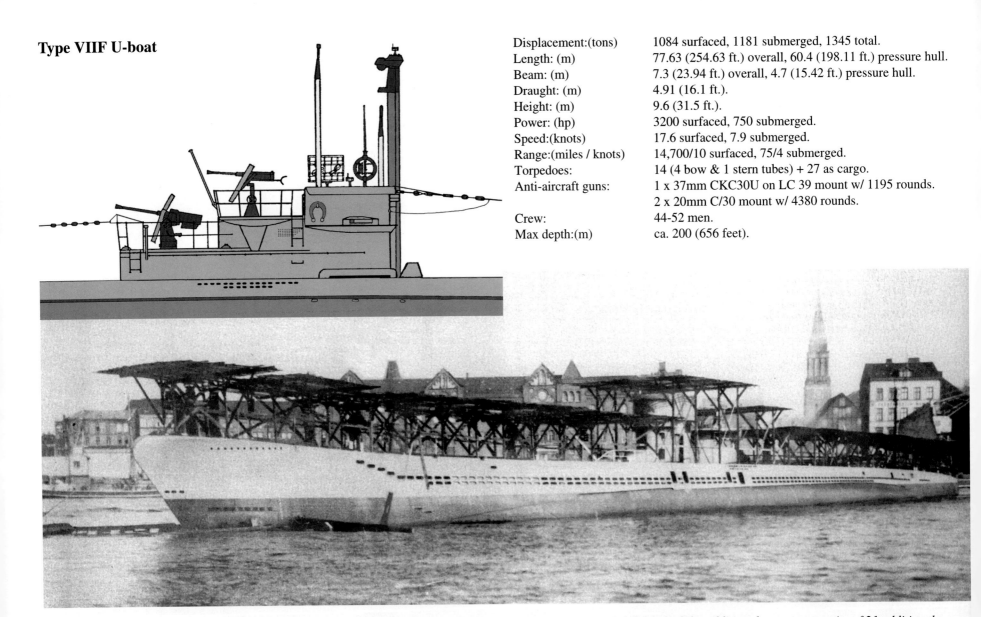

Displacement:(tons)	1084 surfaced, 1181 submerged, 1345 total.
Length: (m)	77.63 (254.63 ft.) overall, 60.4 (198.11 ft.) pressure hull.
Beam: (m)	7.3 (23.94 ft.) overall, 4.7 (15.42 ft.) pressure hull.
Draught: (m)	4.91 (16.1 ft.).
Height: (m)	9.6 (31.5 ft.).
Power: (hp)	3200 surfaced, 750 submerged.
Speed:(knots)	17.6 surfaced, 7.9 submerged.
Range:(miles / knots)	14,700/10 surfaced, 75/4 submerged.
Torpedoes:	14 (4 bow & 1 stern tubes) + 27 as cargo.
Anti-aircraft guns:	1 x 37mm CKC30U on LC 39 mount w/ 1195 rounds.
	2 x 20mm C/30 mount w/ 4380 rounds.
Crew:	44-52 men.
Max depth:(m)	ca. 200 (656 feet).

The Type VIIF U-boat was designed much the same as the VIID, in that they too were an evolution of the standard Type VIIC submarine. These boats were designed to be supply vessels. The design was completed in 1941, with the first boat commissioned in 1943. The torpedo storage compartment added amidships was constructed very similar to that of the VIID. By the time they were ready for service, about March 1943 due to teething problems, they could not be used due to the extensive Allied air cover over the Atlantic, so they were used as combat boats. As designed they carried the normal 14 torpedoes as a VIIC did, but had the additional storage capacity of 21 additional torpedoes in the added cargo room, plus two more in special watertight containers fitted to the deck aft of the conning tower. These boats were initially fitted with a pair of 20mm single mounts on a widened conning tower platform and a single 37mm AA gun on an aft platform extension. These boats also came equipped with a schnorkel.

U-1060 *is about to be launched in the photo to the left. Above is another image of U-1060, possibly following her surrender, showing the conning tower configuration. Below, British Royal Navy officers examine the torpedo plotting control on the conning tower of* U-1060 *after her surrender.*

The first radar fitted to a U-boat was the FuMO-29 "Seetakt", initially installed on a few of the Type IX U-boats bound for the Far East. One of the first Type VII U-boats to receive this radar is pictured here on U-231, a Type VIIC boat. This system was a surface search radar with the fixed antenna fitted to the face of the conning tower. The antenna was a series of two rows of six dipoles per row, twelve total, mounted on a curved plate, which conformed to the face of the conning tower. To achieve a 360° sweep with the radar the U-boat had to motor in a circle. Range was up to 3.5 miles and accuracy was only within 5°, with a field of view of 60°. This was first installed sometime in mid-1941, but was used at least until the end of 1942, as seen in the photograph to the left, dated from December of that year.

The limitations of this set immediately led to the development of an improved system and antenna which rotated, giving 360° coverage and was retractable into the side of a modified conning tower shield. This system was known as FuMO-30. The size of the antenna was 1.4 x 1 meter and had a slightly greater range of 4 miles. One of these antennas is pictured in the image in the lower left of the following page.

All of the Type VII U-boats were equipped from the very first submarine of the class with a radio direction finder. The antenna for this system was a large round loop on a poll, pictured in the photograph to the right, which was retractable into the shield of the conning tower. This antenna rotated 360°, giving all-round coverage.

The antenna in the small inset image below and the image to the far right is for the FuMB-1 "Metox", also known as the "Biscay Cross" radar detector. These were a stop-gap measure that was first installed in August 1942 to detect radar emissions from Allied submarine hunting aircraft. This worked for a short time, until the British realized the Germans had this device and then used it against them by honing in on the slight emission that the antenna itself put out. The antenna was a crudely constructed affair of wood and wire and had to be rotated by hand. Each time the submarine dived, the antenna had to be taken inside the U-boat.

The object in the photograph below is an image of a very rare hydrophone gondola or pod, on U-1105, a Type VIIC/41. This was a very sophisticated system of 24 listening devices arrayed in a semi-circular pod, which was flared into the underside of the bow on only a few of the Type VII boats towards the end of the war. This gave a 300° range of "view" to the submarine and was very accurate, even at long distances. This system was known as "Balkon Gerät" (balcony device). Normally the hydrophones were fitted in the side of the hull, as seen on page 27, but the "view" was limited to about 100° to each side of the boat, with "blind" spots fore and aft.

This image is of the command platform atop the conning tower of U-776, after her surrender in May 1945. The large slot in the port side of the conning tower shield was for the FuMO-61 surface and air search radar antenna, which was an improved version of FuMO-30, with better range and accuracy. The small round antenna on the right side of this photo was for the FuMB-7 "Naxos" radar detector system, an improved version of FuMB-3 "Bali" with two dipoles instead of one.

Both of the photographs on this page are of U-249 upon her surrender to British forces in May 1945. What is important about these two images is the very seldom seen antenna for the FuMB-35 "Athos" radar detection system. The antenna mounted atop a fixed mast, was a hindrance to the submarines performance while submerged. The large slot in the shield of the conning tower was for the FuMO-61 surface and air search retractable radar antenna.

Schnorkel

When Germany invaded the Netherlands, they found a device that the Dutch Navy was experimenting with to run their diesel engines underwater. German scientists paid little attention to this until U-boats were being sunk at an alarming rate. They modified the design to also allow fresh air to be brought into the boat, as well as run the diesel engines, all while under water. This work began in the early months of 1943, but widespread installations were not implemented until early 1944. This device did help the U-boats survive a little longer, but while using the schnorkel, they were essentially blind, therefore the device was used under the cover of darkness. Pictured on this page are various forms of the schnorkel that were used on the Type VII U-boats. The device folded down into the deck when not in use. As Allied radar became more sophisticated, a rubberized, anti-radar matt was applied to the schnorkel head to avoid detection.

The schnorkel head pictured above not only had the radar absorbing rubber matting, but also a "Naxos" all-round radar detection antenna mounted directly on top. This helped to eliminate "blindness" when running with the schnorkel.

Allied aircraft took a large toll against the U-boats, and these two photos are a good example of what an attack upon a submarine looked like. The main photo shows a U-boat caught on the surface recharging her batteries and being bombed and strafed with machine gun fire. The inset photo shows U-625 sinking after being caught on the surface and hit by bombs from an Allied patrol plane.

U-249 surrendering to British Coastal Command aircraft in May 1945.

U-boats surrendering at Wilhelmshaven in May 1945.

Conning tower and foredeck of Type VIIC. This type was used in large numbers against Allied shipping during the war. Note anti-aircraft guns. Also note slot in deck in which Schnorchel mast lies. This type of Schnorchel is raised like an arm on a hinge. Hinge is at aft end of slot. Twin propellers are each driven by a direct connected diesel engine of 1500 hp at 470 rpm and by a direct connected, double unit, d-c electric motor. The Germans say aircraft and radar cut down the effectiveness of these boats and that they are too slow when submerged.

This photograph was found in a file from the US Naval Technical Mission to Europe files in the US National Archives.

A large group of Type VIIC and C/41 U-boats surrender at Wilhelmshaven in May 1945. Note the slight differences between the boats in the foreground.

Type VII U-boats • Location & Date Constructed

Hull Number	Type	Shipyard	Build Period
U-27 - U-32	VII	AG Weser, Bremen	1935 - 1937
U-33 - U-36	VII	Germaniawerft, Kiel	1935 - 1936
U-45 - U-55	VIIB	Germaniawerft, Kiel	1936 - 1939
U-69 - U-72	VIIC	Germaniawerft, Kiel	1938 - 1941
U-73 - U-76	VIIB	Bremer Vulkan, Bremen-Vegesack	1938 - 1940
U-77 - U-82	VIIC	Bremer Vulkan, Bremen-Vegesack	1939 - 1941
U-83 - U-87	VIIB	Flender-Werke, Lübeck	1938 - 1941
U-88 - U-92	VIIC	Flender-Werke, Lübeck	1939 - 1942
U-93 - U-98	VIIC	Germaniawerft, Kiel	1938 - 1940
U-99 - U-102	VIIB	Germaniawerft, Kiel	1937 - 1940
U-132 - U-136	VIIC	Bremer Vulkan, Bremen-Vegesack	1939 - 1941
U-201 - U-212	VIIC	Germaniawerft, Kiel	1939 - 1942
U-213 - U-218	VIID	Germaniawerft, Kiel	1940 - 1942
U-221 - U-232	VIIC	Germaniawerft, Kiel	1940 - 1942
U-235 - U-250	VIIC	Germaniawerft, Kiel	1941 - 1943
U-251 - U-291	VIIC	Bremer Vulkan, Bremen-Vegesack	1939 - 1943
U-292 - U-300	VIIC/41	Bremer Vulkan, Bremen-Vegesack	1941 - 1943
U-301 - U-316	VIIC	Flender-Werke, Lübeck	1940 - 1943
U-317 - U-328	VIIC/41	Flender-Werke, Lübeck	1941 - 1944
U-331 - U-350	VIIC	Nordseewerke, Emden	1939 - 1943
U-351 - U-370	VIIC	Flensburger Schiffsbau, Flensburg	1939 - 1943
U-371 - U-394	VIIC	Howaldtswerke, Kiel	1939 - 1943
U-396 - U-400	VIIC	Howaldtswerke, Kiel	1941
U-401 - U-430	VIIC	Danziger Werft, Danzig	1939 - 1943
U-431 - U-450	VIIC	F. Schichau, Danzig	1939 - 1942
U-451 - U-458	VIIC	Deutsche Werke, Kiel	1939 - 1941
U-465 - U-473	VIIC	Deutsche Werke, Kiel	1940 - 1943
U-475 - U-486	VIIC	Deutsche Werke, Kiel	1941 - 1944
U-551 - U-650	VIIC	Blohm & Voss, Hamburg	1939 - 1942
U-651 - U-683	VIIC	Howaldtswerke, Hamburg	1939 - 1944
U-699 - U-700	VIIC/42	Howaldtswerke, Hamburg	Not Completed
U-701 - U-722	VIIC	HC Stülcken, Hamburg	1939 - 1943
U-731 - U-750	VIIC	F. Schichau, Danzig	1940 - 1943
U-751 - U-768	VIIC	Kriegsmarinewerft, Wilhelmshaven	1939 - 1943
U-771 - U-779	VIIC	Kriegsmarinewerft, Wilhelmshaven	1940 - 1944
U-783 - U-790	VIIC/42	Kriegsmarinewerft, Wilhelmshaven	Not Built
U-821 - U-822	VIIC	Oderwerke, Stettin	1941 - 1944
U-825 - U-826	VIIC	F. Schichau, Danzig	1942 - 1944
U-827 - U-828	VIIC/41	F. Schichau, Danzig	1942 - 1944
U-901	VIIC	Vulcan, Stettin	1941 - 1944
U-903 - U-904	VIIC	Flender-Werke, Lübeck	1942 - 1943
U-905	VIIC	HC Stülcken, Hamburg	1942 - 1943
U-907	VIIC	HC Stülcken, Hamburg	1942 - 1943
U-913 - U-918	VIIC/42	HC Stülcken, Hamburg	Not Built

Hull Number	Type	Shipyard	Build Period
U-921 - U-928	VIIC	Neptun Werft AG, Rostock	1941 - 1944
U-929 - U-930	VIIC/41	Neptun Werft AG, Rostock	1942 - 1944
U-937 - U-942	VIIC/42	AG Neptun, Rostock	Not Built
U-951 - U-994	VIIC	Blohm & Voss, Hamburg	1941 - 1943
U-995	VIIC/41	Blohm & Voss, Hamburg	1941 - 1944
U-997 - U-1010	VIIC/41	Blohm & Voss, Hamburg	1941 - 1944
U-1013 - U-1025	VIIC/41	Blohm & Voss, Hamburg	1942 - 1945
U-1051 - U-1058	VIIC	Germaniawerft, Kiel	1941 - 1944
U-1059 - U-1062	VIIF	Germaniawerft, Kiel	1941 - 1943
U-1063 - U-1065	VIIC/41	Germaniawerft, Kiel	1941 - 1944
U-1069 - U-1080	VIIC/42	Germaniawerft AG, Kiel	Not Completed
U-1093 - U-1100	VIIC/42	Germaniawerft AG, Kiel	Not Completed
U-1101 - U-1102	VIIC	Nordseewerke, Emden	1941 - 1944
U-1103 - U-1110	VIIC/41	Nordseewerke, Emden	1941 - 1944
U-1115 - U-1120	VIIC/42	Nordseewerke, Emden	Not Completed
U-1131 - U-1132	VIIC	Howaldtswerke, Kiel	1941 - 1944
U-1147 - U-1152	VIIC/42	Howaldtswerke, Kiel	Not Built
U-1161 - U-1162	VIIC	Danziger Werft, Danzig	1941 - 1943
U-1163 - U-1172	VIIC/41	Danziger Werft, Danzig	1941 - 1944
U-1191 - U-1210	VIIC	F. Schichau, Danzig	1942 - 1944
U-1215 - U-1220	VIIC/42	F. Schichau GmbH, Danzig	Not Built
U-1271 - U-1279	VIIC/41	Bremer Vulkan, Bremen-Vegesack	1942 - 1944
U-1292 - U-1297	VIIC/42	Vegesacker Werft, Vegesack	Not Built
U-1301 - U-1308	VIIC/41	Flensburger Schiffsbau, Flensburg	1942 - 1945
U-1313 - U-1318	VIIC/42	Flensburger Schiffsbau, Flensburg	Not Built
U-1339 - U-1350	VIIC/42	Flender-Werke AG, Lübeck	Not Built
U-1423 - U-1434	VIIC/42	Blohm & Voss, Hamburg	Not Built
U-1440 - U-1463	VIIC/42	Blohm & Voss, Hamburg	Not Built
U-1805 - U-1822	VIIC/42	Danziger Werft AG, Danzig	Not Built
U-1901 - U-1904	VIIC/42	Kriegsmarinewerft, Wilhelmshaven	Not Built
U-2001 - U-2004	VIIC/42	Howaldtswerke, Hamburg	Not Built
U-2101 - U-2104	VIIC/42	Germaniawerft AG, Kiel	Not Built
U-2301 - U-2318	VIIC/42	F. Schichau GmbH, Danzig	Not Built

Type	Years Built	Number Built	Survived War
VII	1935-1937	10	2 (scuttled at end of war)
VIIB	1936-1941	24	4 (3 scuttled at end of war)
VIIC	1938-1944	593	136 (50 scuttled at end of war)
VIIC/41	1941-1945	70 (88 contracted)	44 (18 scuttled at end of war)
VIIC/42	1943-	0 (all 176 cancelled)	0
VIID	1940-1942	6	1
VIIF	1941-1943	4	1
Total		**707**	**188** (73 out of 188 total were scuttled at the cessation of hostilities)

REFERENCES

The Battle of the Atlantic
T. Hughes & J. Costello, Dial Press, 1977
Conway's All the World's Fighting Ships 1922-1946
R. Chesneau, Conway Maritime Press, 1979
German Warships of the Second World War
H. T. Lenton, Arco Publishing Co., 1975
The German Navy in World War Two
J. P. M. Showell, Naval Institute Press., 1979
Naval Radar
N. Friedman, Conway Maritime Press, 1988
Naval Weapons of WWII
J. Campbell, Conway Maritime Press, 1985
The U-boat
E. Rössler, Arms & Armour Press, 1981
The Type VII U-boat
R. Westwood, Naval Institute Press, 1984
Type VII U-boats
R. C. Stern, Arms & Armour Press, 1991

RESOURCES

U. S. Naval Historical Center
Building 57, 805 Kidder Breese St. SE,
Washington Navy Yard, Washington DC, 20374-2571
(202)433-2765 • Web site: www.history.navy.mil

U. S. National Archives
8601 Adelphi Rd., College Park, MD. 20740-6001
(301)713-6800 • Web site: www.nara.gov

U. S. Naval Institute
291 Wood Rd., Annapolis, MD 21402-5034
(800)233-8764 • Web site: www.usni.org

Snyder & Short Enterprises
PMB 224, 9175 Kiefer Blvd., Sacramento, CA. 95826-5105
Web site: www.shipcamouflage.com

ACKNOWLEDGMENTS
Classic Warships
would like to express its gratitude to the following individuals
Don Montgomery • Steve Barker
Patrick Toussaint • John Asmussen
Don Preul & Jeanne Pollard
Ed Finney, Rob Hanshew & Chuck Haberlein, Jr.
@ US Naval Historical Center
All the nice ladies on the 5th. floor @ Archives II

WARSHIP PICTORIAL SERIES
available at the time of this printing
W. P. # 4 USS Texas BB-35
W. P. # 7 New Orleans Class Cruisers
W. P. # 9 Yorktown Class Carriers
W. P. #10 Indianapolis & Portland
W. P. #12 Benson/Gleaves Class Destroyers
W. P. #14 USS Wichita CA-45
W. P. #17 IJN Myoko Class Cruisers
W. P. #18 USS New Mexico BB-40
W. P. #19 KM Bismarck
W. P. #20 HMS Hood
W. P. #21 KM Prinz Eugen
W. P. #22 USS Ticonderoga CV/CVA/CVS-14
W. P. #23 Italian Heavy Cruisers of WWII
W. P. #25 IJN Yamato Class Battleships
W. P. #27 KM Type VII U-Boats

Front Cover: U-253 *at the Baltic Sea port of Hela, Poland, April or May 1942.*

Back Cover: *The image to the right is of a few type VII U-boats at Hela in May 1942. The image to the left was from one of the covers of the Nazi era propaganda magazine "Die Wehrmacht".*

The image to the left is of the Italian Royal Navy heavy cruiser Fiume *at Venice, Italy about 1939 and is one of the subjects of Warship Pictorial #23 - Italian Heavy Cruisers of WWII.*